My GRANDPA Had a STROKE

Published by
MAGINATION PRESS
An Educational Publishing Foundation Book
American Psychological Association
750 First Street, NE
Washington, DC 20002

For more information about our books, including a complete catalog,
please write to us, call 1-800-374-2721,
or visit our website at www.maginationpress.com.

Editor: Darcie Conner Johnston
Art Director: Susan K. White
Printed by Worzalla, Stevens Point, Wisconsin

Library of Congress Cataloging-in-Publication Data

Butler, Dori Hillestad.
My grandpa had a stroke / by Dori Hillestad Butler ; illustrated by Nicole Wong.
p. cm.
Summary: "With his parents' help, young Ryan learns about his grandfather's
stroke and how it will affect both his grandfather and his family."
ISBN-10: 1-59147-806-5 (hardcover : alk. paper)
ISBN-10: 1-59147-807-3 (pbk. : alk. paper)
ISBN-13: 978-1-59147-806-5 (hardcover : alk. paper)
ISBN-13: 978-1-59147-807-2 (pbk. : alk. paper)
1. Cerebrovascular disease—Juvenile literature. I. Wong, Nicole, ill. II. Title.
RC388.5.B88 2007
616.8'1—dc22   2006034528

10 9 8 7 6 5 4 3 2 1

My GRANDPA Had a STROKE

written by Dori Hillestad Butler

illustrated by Nicole Wong

MAGINATION PRESS • WASHINGTON, D.C.

My Grandpa Joe is crazy about fishing. Can you tell? He bought this house on Hall Lake just so he could go fishing every day.

I like fishing, too. So every Saturday, Grandpa picks me up in his truck. We stop at Morrie's Diner for breakfast. We get bait there, too. Then we go to Grandpa's house, get in the boat, and zoom across the lake to Grandpa's favorite fishing spot.

I know what to do because Grandpa
taught me how to bait my hook, how to cast my
line, and how to sit quiet so we don't scare the fish.

Some Saturdays we're out for a long time,
and we don't catch anything. It's not as fun when
we don't catch anything.

Then Grandpa says, "Patience, Ryan.
Good things come to those who wait."

Other Saturdays I catch a fish so big that Grandpa has to help me reel it in. I wish every Saturday could be like that. Grandpa says he wishes so, too.

But one Saturday Grandpa can't come for me. Dad says that Grandpa had a stroke. He's in the hospital, and Mom is with him.

"What's a stroke?" I ask.

"It's something that can happen inside a person's brain," says Dad. "Usually it only happens to an older person, like Grandpa. What happens is part of the brain stops working the way it's supposed to. Then the person can't do some things the way he could before."

"Did part of Grandpa's brain stop working?" I ask.

"Yes. Grandpa's stroke happened in the part of the brain that tells him to move the left side of his body. So now he can't move his left arm or his left leg. Sometimes people who have strokes can't talk, because their stroke happened in the talking part of the brain. Sometimes they can't think like they used to, because it happened in the thinking part of the brain. Grandpa's been sleeping since the stroke happened, so we don't know everything he can and cannot do yet."

I am worried about my grandpa.
I want to see him.

"You can see Grandpa when he
wakes up," says Dad.

Grandpa sleeps and sleeps.
Finally, during dinner on Monday,
Mom calls and says Grandpa is awake.
And he's asking for me!

Dad drives us to the hospital, and we walk
down a long hallway until we find Grandpa's room.
Grandpa is sitting up in bed with pillows all
around him. He looks tired.

"Hello…Ryan," he says slowly.

My insides feel funny. That old man in the bed doesn't look like my grandpa. He isn't wearing his fishing hat or his glasses. And his mouth looks funny, like someone pasted it on crooked.

Grandpa holds his arm out to hug me, so I go over and hug him. But he only hugs me back with one hand. His other hand just lies there.

The doctor comes in and asks Grandpa to raise his left arm. Grandpa's arm stays still.

"Can you move that arm at all?" the doctor asks.

"It's moving," Grandpa says. But it's not.

The doctor tickles Grandpa's foot. I curl my toes, because Grandpa always tickles my foot if I don't have slippers on.

"Do you feel that?" the doctor asks.

Grandpa doesn't answer. He is asleep again.

Dad touches my shoulder.

"It's time for us to go," he whispers.

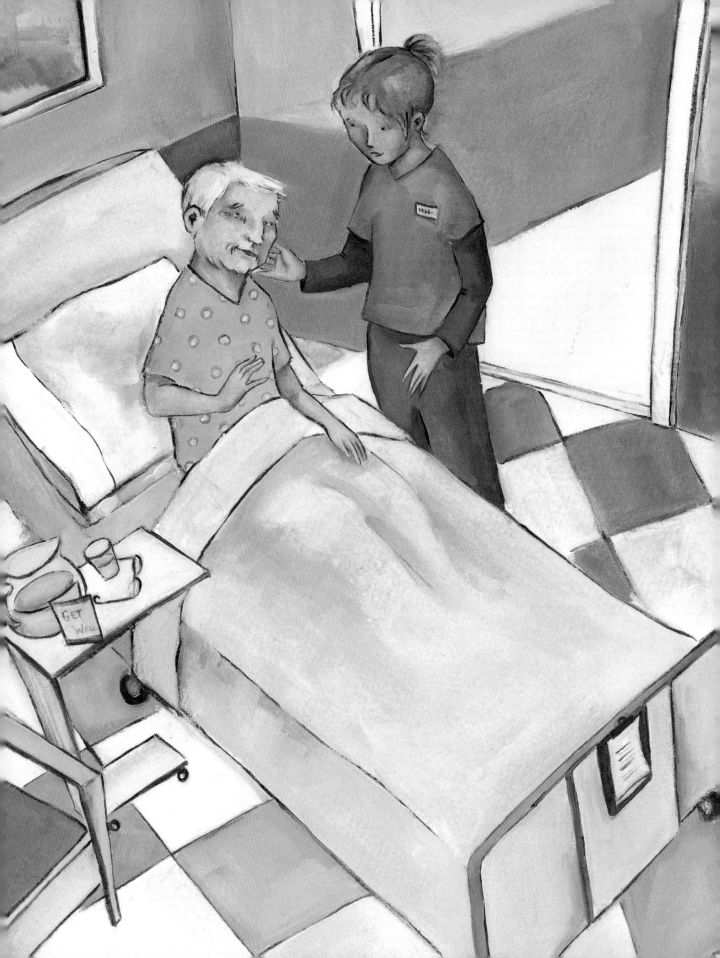

The next time I visit Grandpa, there's a nice lady in his room. She has a nametag that says "Kari." Mom tells me she's called a physical therapist, and she's going to help Grandpa move his body better.

First she tries to help Grandpa sit up by himself. But every time she lets go of him, he falls to the side.

"Your grandpa needs to learn how to hold himself up straight again," Kari says. "Because of the stroke, he can't tell that he's leaning to one side. The first step in getting better is learning to sit straight."

I don't like to see my big, strong Grandpa like this.
He's like a baby. He can't sit or stand or feed himself.
He can't even go to the bathroom by himself. Grandpa
also cries. I don't like it when grown-ups cry.

Mom says grown-ups cry when they're sad, just
like kids do. She says people also cry when they're mad.
Probably Grandpa is both sad and mad about the things
he can't do right now. Mom says that she cries about
Grandpa's stroke, too. But crying is okay, and Grandpa
is getting better.

A few days later, Grandpa leaves the hospital and goes to stay in a different place. Mom and Dad call it a rehabilitation center. People there give Grandpa exercises to do. They help him practice sitting straight and standing up. They even help him walk a little. Grandpa can't move his left leg very well, so somebody has to scoot his left foot forward for him.

One day I notice something funny about Grandpa. "Hey, Grandpa!" I say. "You only combed one side of your hair, and you only shaved one side of your face."

Grandpa squints at himself in the mirror. "Hmm," he says. "Guess I forgot." Then he combs the other side of his hair and shaves the other side of his face.

Another day, a big lady walks past Grandpa's room.
Grandpa calls out, "Hey, Fatty!" and laughs like a little kid.

I have never heard Grandpa say such a mean thing before.

Mom says that sometimes people who have had a stroke
say things they wouldn't normally say.

21

Grandpa looks and acts so different now that
sometimes I don't want to go see him. "I'll visit him when
he's back to the way he used to be," I tell Mom.

    Mom reaches for my hand. "Grandpa may never be
the way he used to be, Ryan. But he's still your grandpa.
And he still loves you. The stroke will never change that."

    I love my grandpa, too. So I keep visiting him.
Even though it's hard.

A few weeks go by. Grandpa is better, but he still can't walk very well by himself. And his arm is still in that funny position.

The doctor says there isn't any more they can do for Grandpa at the rehabilitation center. It's time for him to leave.

"Where will he go?" I ask. He can't go back to his house. He can't take care of himself.

"He'll come live with us," Mom says.

I would've been happy to have Grandpa come live with us before the stroke. But now I'm scared. What if he falls down? What if we forget to give him his medicine?

"Do we know how to take care of him?" I ask.

"Dad and I will learn," Mom says. "And you'll probably find a couple of ways to help Grandpa feel at home."

Mom and Dad get the guest room ready
for Grandpa, and I help. We take off the door
so Grandpa's wheelchair will fit. We pick up all
the rugs in the hallways. We put hand rails in
the bathroom, and we build a ramp out front.
Now I can rollerblade right out my door!

At first, Grandpa doesn't seem very happy
at our house. All he wants to do is watch TV.

I think I know how to cheer Grandpa up.

"Hey, Grandpa," I say. "Today's Saturday.
We should go fishing."

Grandpa looks at me. "Can't," he says.

"Why not?" I ask.

"Can't walk. Can't move my arm," Grandpa says.

But Mom and I help Grandpa get into the car.
We stop at Morrie's Diner for breakfast.
Then we drive out to Grandpa's place.

Grandpa can't get in his boat. But we can wheel him on the dock. And we can go fishing right there.

I bait Grandpa's hook, just like he showed me.
I cast Grandpa's line, just like he showed me.
And then we wait. Because good things come to those who wait.

Before long, Grandpa has a fish.
I help him reel it in.

Grandpa is smiling. "We did it!" he says.
I wish every Saturday could be like this.
Maybe it can.

Note to Parents

Strokes are the number one cause of disability in the United States, affecting more than 600,000 people every year. Depending on its location in the brain, a stroke can cause cognitive, emotional, or personality changes, as well as physical disability. When a stroke occurs, families of its victims may be faced with learning to cope with many of these changes. Even young children need to be informed and helped to adjust, especially when they have enjoyed a close relationship with the stroke victim. Because the chance of stroke increases with age, the victim is often a grandparent.

EXPLAINING THE STROKE

Explaining a stroke to a grandchild requires honesty and sensitivity. Children should be told immediately, but parents do well by keeping the explanation simple, as Ryan's father does in *My Grandpa Had a Stroke*. Listen carefully to their questions. Follow their lead in terms of what they want to know. (Often what a child is curious about is very different from what concerns an adult.) Answer questions calmly, and provide a level of information that is appropriate for your child's age and temperament. It is not necessary to share most details. For example, you might say, "Because of the stroke, Grandpa can't walk or do things with his arm right now. We won't know for awhile how much he can and can't do. But the doctors are taking good care of him."

For adult family members, the hardest part may be coping with a lack of information and waiting for all the effects to show themselves. Avoid sharing your fears and speculation, but do tell your children the basic facts and acknowledge your obvious feelings. Concealing or minimizing them can backfire, because children may imagine the worst when they see their parents' distress or when family routines are significantly disrupted.

If your child observes your own natural upset, it's helpful to say, for example, "I am sad because of Grandpa's stroke and the things he can't do now. This is hard for all of us. But we know the doctors are doing a good job taking care of him, and he is getting a little better every day." This kind of honesty is reassuring for children. It also shows them how to express their own feelings in a healthy way and gives them "permission" to do so.

CHILDREN'S FEELINGS AND REACTIONS

Children may feel any combination of sadness, worry, confusion, and anger. Witnessing the changes in their grandparent, who may have been healthy and active a few days or weeks ago, is upsetting. Now he (or she) may be unable to walk unassisted or speak clearly or feed himself. His face may look different because his facial muscles aren't working normally. He may even seem like a different person altogether.

At first, children may be afraid or uncomfortable and not want to be close to their grandparent or hug him. This is a normal response. Address these feelings and help your child work through them by saying, for example, "You're probably a little scared, seeing Grandpa so different. That's okay. It may take a little while to get used to the changes." In the meantime, avoid forcing your child if he or she is clearly uncomfortable.

Younger children may have a hard time understanding when the changes are permanent, and will want to know when Grandpa will get better. "Grandpa will probably get a little better, but he will never be able to walk the way he used to," or "Grandmom may never be able to talk the way she used to, but she can listen to us and look at your pictures, and we'll learn other ways to find out what she wants to say" are helpful reminders.

Older children may feel angry, as well as sad and worried—especially if the grandparent and child shared a special bond. A loss such as this feels very unfair ("Why did this have to happen to *my* grandfather?"), and children will need to mourn the loss of the relationship as it was. Allow them plenty of room to talk about the things they miss, and help them think of new ways to be with the grandparent.

In addition, the stroke may have changed the child's own daily life. Parents may need to spend a lot of time with the grandparent. They may also be tired, distressed, and distracted, which makes them less emotionally available. And family activities may be curtailed. Young children normally think of their own needs first and may need help understanding the more urgent needs of others: for example, "I know you are frustrated that I have to be at the hospital again. I miss you too. Things will be more normal soon, but right now Grandmom really needs my help."

If kids are angry that the world is no longer as predictable as it seemed, they are also scared. Most children are afraid of illness, and they may worry about death. Offer realistic reassurances, such as, "Grandpa will never be the way he used to be, but we hope he will get better." Let your child know that no one can catch a stroke and that none of you are in any danger. You might say, "I know you're worried that I might have a stroke like your grandfather. You should know that no one can catch a stroke, and that I expect the rest of us to be fine for a long, long time."

Less obvious than physical effects of the stroke are changes in personality and cognitive ability. Because they are not visible, they can be quite confusing for the young child. A grandparent may say something that doesn't make sense, behave impulsively, have problems with memory or attention, be confused about time or space, or even lose some awareness of his body.

As parents realize that the stroke victim is facing such challenges, it's best to inform children: "Because of the stroke, Grandpa can't think the way he used to, and sometimes he doesn't realize what he's saying" or "sometimes he forgets about the left side of his body," as appropriate. If these problems surface when your child is with his grandparent, calmly remind him that the behavior is a result of the stroke: "The stroke is causing Grandpa to forget about the left side of his body" or "Grandpa said that to that lady because his brain isn't working correctly right now." When possible, include the grandparent in the conversation: "Dad, you probably don't realize that you shaved just half of your face. Would you like to do the other side?" It's important to show your child that the grandparent, despite the limitations caused by the stroke, still possesses all of his humanity and will be treated with the same love and respect as before.

WHAT PARENTS CAN DO

Children do well when they are encouraged to talk about their feelings and to ask questions. In this way, they are best able to work through their confusion, anger, fears, and grief. Be receptive, and take the time to listen. Answer questions, as appropriate, and encourage optimism. And reassure them that their feelings are normal, while commending their efforts to cope. For example, you might say, "It's okay to feel angry that Grandpa can't take you fishing anymore. Most kids would feel the same way. It doesn't mean you don't love him," or "I know it's hard that I have to spend so much time at the center with Grandma. I am really proud of the way you have been able to manage. And the cards and pictures you've made for her have helped her feel so much better."

It is also helpful for children when their parents maintain sameness in daily routines and expectations of their children's behavior. Bedtime, mealtimes, homework, chores, family rituals, discipline, and such should all proceed as normally as possible. The more predictable and stable the world seems, the easier it will be for the child to cope with the changes that are unavoidable.

In the immediate aftermath of the stroke, parents will want to be cautious in deciding whether a child may visit a grandparent. After considering the child's age and temperament, as well as the stability of the grandparent's physical and emotional condition, you might decide your child is ready and whether there is an adult who can accompany the child and remain calm and attentive to the child's needs. If so, plan a time when the grandparent is awake and in the best possible spirits, and limit the visit to a few minutes. If it's too soon to visit, children can stay connected by drawing pictures, making cards, and writing or dictating notes. Phone calls are also appropriate if the grandparent's speech is not more than mildly impaired.

Once the effects of the stroke are fully known and the grandparent is at home or in long-term care, help your child find activities to share with his or her grandparent. Reading, listening to music, or even watching television together can be rewarding.

If your child is resistant, you might say, "I know it's hard to be with Grandmom when she seems so different. Let's think of some ways that make it easier for you." Build on your child's ideas, or offer some of your own, such as inviting Grandmom to a game or a movie so that they can be together without having to talk so much.

If the grandparent comes to live with you, prepare your children as much as possible. Discuss important details in advance, such as where Grandpa will sleep, what accommodations he needs, and who will take care of him. Children will also need to know how this will change their lives and what their own role will be. Reassure

them that while there will indeed be changes, they will still be "children" who will continue to do all the things they used to. It is the job of the parents and any professionals to make sure Grandpa's needs are met. At the same time, it's important that children and grandparents develop ways to spend time together, as Ryan does in this story. And it is vital that parents provide any extra comfort and support to their children as they adjust to the new member of the household.

At the same time, parents need relief and support themselves. Seek help and information from local groups and national organizations such as the American Stroke Association and the National Stroke Association. If you or any of your children need more help coping with changes, feelings, or demands, don't hesitate to consult with a therapist or other mental health professional with experience working with families facing illness.

Children are resilient. By including them appropriately and by helping them respond in healthy and constructive ways, parents not only help them cope but also give them skills that will benefit them throughout their lives.

About the Author

DORI HILLESTAD BUTLER is an award-winning author of many children's books. "When my father suffered a stroke, I was desperate for a book to read with my young children but couldn't find what I was looking for. So I wrote it," she says. She lives with her family in Iowa.

About the Illustrator

NICOLE WONG is a graduate of the Rhode Island School of Design. Her illustrations have been featured in many children's books, magazines, and greeting cards. She lives with her husband and their dog and cat in Massachusetts.